S0-AZK-836

THE CURRIER GALLERY OF ART

A History

1929-1989

by

Aurore Dionne Eaton

29132

Table of Contents

FOREWORD AND ACKNOWLEDGMENTS

On the occasion of the Sixtieth Anniversary of The Currier Gallery of Art, we are pleased to present the history of the museum. With this publication, we honor the Currier's progress and achievements as well as those who have been instrumental in making these accomplishments possible.

Aurore Dionne Eaton has turned sixty years of primary source material, never before organized as a history, into a highly informative narrative. She contributed far more time than was originally anticipated in her dedication to making the history accurate and complete, and she maintained her enthusiasm throughout this challenging project. Her dedication and enthusiasm come from her love for the Currier Gallery, which she says goes back to her first visit as a freshman in high school. What is indeed remarkable is that Eaton's devotion is not the exception, but rather is characteristic of the volunteers and staff who, through the years, have given their time out of love for this great institution. We thank Eaton as well as all those who have given so much in their affection for The Currier Gallery of Art.

The publication of the history would not have been possible without the help of many people. Our appreciation is extended especially to Maria K. Graubart, librarian and archivist of the Currier, who guided the research and editing of the manuscript. Librarians who also assisted Eaton in her research include William N. Copeley, librarian of the New Hampshire Historical Society, Concord; Elizabeth Lessard, librarian of the Manchester Historic Association; and the librarians of the New Hampshire Room and periodicals section of the Manchester City Library.

Curator emeritus Melvin E. Watts generously provided invaluable oral history and answered many questions, as did trustees and former directors. Research on the early trustees was based on data previously assembled by trustee emerita Mary Shaw Shirley. We are indebted to numerous others who also contributed valuable information. Thanks are due to Julie A. Solz for research assistance, Inez McDermott for editorial assistance, Virginia H. Eshoo and Linda Landis for copy editing the manuscript, Dawn Goforth for proofing and preparing the final manuscript for press, and Lisa deFrancis and her staff for the tasteful design of this publication. Most of all we wish to thank all our members and patrons, because without them the Currier's distinguished accomplishments would not have been possible.

Kimon S. Zachos
President, Board of Trustees

Marilyn Friedman Hoffman
Director

The Currier Gallery of Art opened its doors for the first time at 8:30 pm on Wednesday, October 9, 1929. The dream of Governor Moody Currier (1806–1898) and his wife Hannah A. Currier (1829–1915) was now a reality. Their city, Manchester, New Hampshire, had a museum of art to enrich the lives of its citizens.

More than 1,400 invited guest crowded into the galleries for the historic evening. Included at the gala reception were dignitaries from the city and the state, as well as prominent artists, critics, and museum professionals from New England and New York. The guests were received at the Orange Street entrance by volunteer ushers and were led into the museum's open court, the center stage of the new institution. There they admired the combined effect of the marble staircases, the columned arcades, the brilliantly colored Renaissance-inspired decor, and the lustrous black and white floor mosaic.

A focal point of the court was the bronze fountain sculpture by American artist Harriet Frishmuth, installed, as it is today, at the south end of the mosaic floor. Entitled *The Crest of the Wave*, the sculpture depicts a graceful nude woman poised to leap with the surf. Two small bronzes, a young man and a young woman, both posed in energetic stride, stood on the newel posts of the stair landing. All three pieces were on loan from the Grand Central Art Galleries of New York.

Fig. 1   Hannah Currier in the gown she wore to the governor's ball at the
Eagle Hotel, Concord, in 1885.

After the guests had absorbed the rich ambience of the court, they were ushered through the galleries and were greeted along the way by the trustees and their spouses. The west gallery on the first floor was organized as a Colonial-era period room with arrangements of early-American furniture, rugs and portraits lent by Manchester residents. The centerpiece was a block-printed early nineteenth-century wallpaper depicting a panoramic view of Lyon, France. The wallpaper, by Felix Sauvenet, had been given to the museum by Hannah Currier's niece, Penelope W. Snow, a museum trustee.

In the first floor east gallery the guests viewed the museum's newly purchased collection of Mesopotamian, Greek, Roman and Renaissance plaster casts. The small gallery off the north side of the court was arranged as a memorial room to Moody and Hannah Currier. The carpeted space contained full-length portraits of the Curriers, furniture from the Currier mansion, and family memorabilia. The northeast gallery was a children's room with antique dolls and doll furniture.

Fine examples of contemporary sculpture and painting, courtesy of Grand Central Art Galleries, graced the second floor. Guests also admired European and American landscape and genre paintings selected from the Currier's first bequest, the collection of George A. Leighton, a Manchester inventor and industrialist.

Throughout the evening the museum's first director, Maud Briggs Knowlton, mingled with the guests. The strains of a chamber music ensemble in the upper court provided the perfect backdrop to toast the future of the new institution.

The sound of music would fill the Currier frequently in the years to come, and the museum's modest permanent collection would grow into a remarkable assemblage of fine and decorative arts. The Currier Gallery of Art would become one of the country's premiere small museums, its importance extending far beyond the boundaries of the city. Moody and Hannah Currier's legacy would prove to be a magnificent tribute to their foresight and generosity.

MOODY AND HANNAH CURRIER

Early in the nineteenth century, the wheels of the industrial revolution were turning in New England. The citizens of the small town of Derryfield, New Hampshire, were swept up by the promises of technological innovation and progress. They envisioned a bright future, one which would be shaped by harnessing the energy of the Merrimack River. In 1810, these citizens changed the name of Derryfield to Manchester, daring to hope that some day their little village could emulate the great British manufacturing center of Manchester.

Indeed, Manchester, New Hampshire, would become one of New England's most prosperous industrial cities. A group of wealthy investors, The Boston Associates, sought to transform Manchester into its version of a utopian industrial society. The Associates bought wide stretches of land on the banks of the Merrimack River in Manchester, and in 1831 incorporated the Amoskeag Manufacturing Company. They chose the old Indian name "Amoskeag" because of its association with an area of rapids and waterfalls on the Merrimack River in Manchester, once a fertile fishing ground.

The fate of the city became inextricably bound to the operations of the Amoskeag. The company controlled the sale of its vast tracts of property, assuring that the pattern of the city's growth was under company control. The Amoskeag's engineer and first agent, Ezekiel A. Straw, laid out the city's streets and parks, planning the main avenue, Elm Street, to run parallel with the long line of mill buildings on the river's bank.

The Amoskeag prospered for the remainder of the nineteenth century and into the early twentieth century, and its vast operations became the largest single textile-producing complex in the world. Other textile factories opened in the city, as well as numerous manufacturing and service industries. As Manchester entered the Victorian era it was already a bustling city, attracting ambitious people who were eager to take advantage of economic and professional opportunities. One of these was Moody Currier.

Moody Currier was born in Boscawen, New Hampshire, in 1806, the illegitimate child of Moody Morse Currier of Hopkinton and Rhoda Putney of Dunbarton. He grew up on the Putney farm in Dunbarton, and worked as a farmhand from an early age. Yearning to be educated, he studied late into the night, even when exhausted after a long day of hard labor. While in his twenties, Currier attended Hopkinton Academy in Hopkinton, New Hampshire, and graduated with high honors from Dartmouth College in Hanover in 1834.

Currier taught school in Concord, New Hampshire, and was an editor of the *New Hampshire Literary Gazette*. He found success as an educator, becoming preceptor of Hopkinton Academy and then master of the Lowell, Massachusetts, high school. In his spare time, he studied law and in 1841 was admitted to the New Hampshire bar. After arriving in Manchester that year, he purchased an interest in the *Manchester Democrat*, and was its part-time editor.

Moody Currier's successful law practice opened doors in the business world. In 1848 he helped found the Amoskeag Bank, and became its first cashier. He was named president of the Amoskeag National Bank, and of the Amoskeag Savings Bank, and developed other interests in the city's thriving banking industry. A director and financial advisor to the New Hampshire Fire Insurance Company, he was also involved in the railroad industry, in manufacturing, and in utilities.

He remained active in commerce until his retirement at the age of 86.

Moody Currier had a second career in politics and was elected to both city and state offices. Originally a Democrat, he joined the newly created Republican Party in 1852, largely because of his anti-slavery beliefs. He was the chairman of the state's war committee at the start of the Civil War, and was responsible for raising and equipping the New Hampshire troops. As a salute to him, the Eighth Regiment christened its encampment in Manchester *Camp Currier*. He was elected governor in 1884, serving in 1885–1886. To this day his state papers are regarded as classics of official literature.

A scholar of both ancient religion and modern theology, conversant in several languages, and an accomplished amateur poet, Currier penned admirable verses which reflected his love of nature and his progressive thinking on spiritual matters. He donated hundreds of books to the Manchester City Library, where he served as a trustee. He was an incorporator of the Manchester Historic Association and a member of the New Hampshire Historical Society.

Neither an artist nor a collector, Currier's interest in art appears to have existed primarily on an abstract, philosophical plane. He possessed a deep appreciation of the role played by art in the development of human civilization. His interest in art was encouraged through his friendship with Henry Herrick, a noted watercolorist and luminary in Manchester social circles. Moody Currier served as a trustee of the Manchester Institute of Arts and Sciences, and was president of the Manchester Art Association for fourteen years, a post which Herrick had previously held.

In his private life, Currier faced a series of tragedies. Illnesses claimed his first two wives and his only daughter. His first wife, Lucretia C. Dustin of Bow, whom he married in 1836, died in 1847. Their daughter Lucretia D. Currier died in 1859 at the age of 19. Currier married his second wife, Mary W. Kidder of Manchester, later in 1847. She died in 1869. Records indicate that she bore a stillborn son in 1850.

Currier's poetry often revealed his responses to his tragic past. In one piece, he relates the dying words of a young woman to her father, as told to a friend. The poem was perhaps inspired by his feelings for his daughter, Lucretia:

> Tell him I'll wake again when morn
> Sweet beams of light shall spread,
> And life's immortal day shall dawn
> Upon the sleeping dead.
>
> Tell him I'll wake in youthful bloom,
> All fresh and fair and bright;
> No fell disease nor sorrow's gloom
> My rising joys shall blight.[1]

Currier married his third wife, Hannah A. Slade, in 1869. Slade was born in Brookfield, Vermont, in 1829. She attended the prestigious Thetford Academy in Vermont, and studied music, French and literature in Boston. She taught public school for several years in Manchester before marrying.

After Moody Currier's death in 1898, Hannah Currier lived a quiet existence, shunning publicity. For several years her niece, Penelope W. Snow, shared the Currier estate with her. "Nellie" Snow was an amateur artist who would later become a trustee and patron of the museum.

The Currier homestead was located in a neighborhood of distinctive private homes in East Manchester, several blocks from the busy commercial center of the city. Each house, with its gardens and stables, occupied an entire city block. Currier constructed his grand brick residence around 1868 on the lot bordered by Orange, Ash, Myrtle and Beech streets. The beautifully landscaped grounds were greatly admired.

Currier had expressed both in life and in his will the desire that his fortune be used for the endowment of an art museum to be located at his Manchester estate. Hannah shared his feelings, and made provisions for the museum in her own will. As Moody and Hannah Currier had no children, The Currier Gallery of Art was to be their legacy to future generations.

Hannah Currier managed her husband's estate wisely so that sufficient funds would be available to establish the museum. After her death in 1915, her will was administered by executor Arthur M. Heard, president of the Amoskeag National Bank. On July 17, 1917, the trustees, including Heard, met for the first time at the offices of the Amoskeag National Bank in Manchester.

The Currier Gallery of Art was officially chartered by a joint act of the New Hampshire State Senate and House of Representatives in 1919.

The Museum is Created

Moody and Hannah Currier left few instructions for their museum. They simply indicated in their wills that it " . . . will be purely a benevolent and public institution," to be administered as a public trust. They also stipulated that the appointed trustees would perform their duties without pay, and that the museum must be located on the site of the Currier mansion. Hannah Currier's will specified that the institution would be named "The Currier Gallery of Art."

The trustees were free to remodel the Currier mansion into a museum or to build a new structure. They ultimately decided to tear down the house and create a new building. They invested the endowment wisely in order to accumulate the necessary funds for the project and began the search for an architect. In 1920 they commissioned the prestigious Boston architect Ralph Adams Cram of the firm of Cram and Ferguson to create a proposal for consideration. Cram was one of the country's most sought-after architects and had achieved fame as a medievalist and philosopher. He executed at least twenty-five drawings for the museum and produced an illustrated booklet explaining his ideas for the design of The Currier Gallery of Art and his theories on museum architecture.

Cram envisioned the museum as an Italian house of the fifteenth century with intimate galleries surrounding a small open court. A prominent element would be a two-story chapel-gallery which would house religious art. For Cram, "A gallery in such a museum would therefore be a livable [sic] room, with furniture, wall hangings, and architectural surroundings such as one might have found at some particular time in the past."[2]

In Cram's museum, the director would enjoy the luxury of a large private office and could retire to a personal study on the floor above. The staff, however, would be allowed virtually no space in which to work. Cram suggested that musical events would be held in the court area, but that an auditorium or other gathering place would not be necessary.

Cram's concept resembled that of the celebrated Isabella Stewart Gardner Museum in Boston, opened in 1903. According to architectural historian Douglass Shand Tucci, "... for Cram there could be no more stimulating a model for a museum than that designed by Mrs. Gardner, whose convictions about art in architecture had long paralleled his own."[3]

After two years of deliberation, the trustees rejected Cram's design in November 1922. No record remains of the reasons for their decision, but it may be speculated that the trustees found that Cram's proposal too much resembled the private domain of a collector and was not practical as a public institution.

The month after Cram's dismissal, another prominent Boston architect, R. Clipston Sturgis, was invited to present an alternative concept to the trustees. He described his concept as follows:

> A Museum should have the home quality, be more like a house than a public building, especially true of a small museum. . . . the exterior, of brick and marble, is in general character like the early brick house of Colonial days. On entering one is in the front hall of a private house, and from this one steps into an 18th Century drawing room, with two fireplaces, and with furniture and paintings of that time.[4]

The trustees were more favorably impressed by this approach, which found its roots in the British heritage of New England. They met several times with Sturgis and by April 1924 had agreed to proceed with the construction of the museum according to his design. By June, Sturgis was seeking construction bids, but later that month the trustees instructed the architect to stop work and await further instructions. He was removed from the project in January 1925. The reason for this change of heart was, once again, left unrecorded. Perhaps the intention of the trustees was to create a more conspicuously public-oriented institution than either Cram or Sturgis had envisioned.

Later in 1925, the trustees turned to another architectural firm, Tilton and Githens of New York City. The two partners, Edward L. Tilton and Alfred M. Githens, had designed a number of successful public buildings throughout the country, and

Tilton had already earned the admiration of Manchester citizens with his grand design for the Carpenter Memorial Library building, completed in 1914. The firm would later design the buildings for the Museum of Fine Arts and the Museum of Natural History (later the Springfield Science Museum) both in Springfield, Massachusetts, as well as the Manchester Historic Association building and other public and commercial structures in Manchester.

After reviewing sketches and tentative plans for the museum, the trustees awarded the commission to Tilton and Githens in May 1926. It is likely that trustee Frank P. Carpenter influenced his fellow board members in this decision. He had worked with Tilton on the library building he had donated to the city and was confident of the architect's abilities. In October 1926, Carpenter, the building committee chairman, was authorized to handle the details of the agreement with the firm. Tilton, who had studied at the Ecole des Beaux-Arts in Paris, was assigned as the principal architect on the project.

Two trustees were appointed in December 1925, an artist and art educator, Maud Briggs Knowlton; and Hannah Currier's niece, Penelope W. Snow. In the following months, Knowlton and Snow traveled around the country together, visiting museums with the purpose of researching the type of institution which would best fit the needs of the city of Manchester. The information they gathered proved helpful to both the architect and the trustees. Although Hannah Currier had left no instructions for the museum, it is believed that her ideas may have been communicated through her long-time companion, Penelope Snow.

Tilton's concept for the new museum was a pleasing Beaux-Arts interpretation of an Italian Renaissance palazzo. He designed a two-story indoor atrium-lit court with Italianate columns and arches. In laying out the design for the galleries, he employed the latest museum exhibition and lighting theories, successfully balancing intimate spaces with open areas, and overcoming the inadequacies of artificial lighting through the careful placement of skylights and windows. He installed working fireplaces of imported marble in four of the galleries, an unexpected feature that introduced an inviting domesticity to the rooms. An ample auditorium served as a multi-purpose gathering place.

In March 1927 L. H. Shattuck, Inc., of Manchester was chosen as the building contractor. The Currier mansion was demolished, and construction work progressed. That fall, Knowlton traveled to New York to meet with the architect to discuss details of the lighting fixtures, mantels, and mosaic work.

The museum structure was solidly built on a granite base, faced with Kentucky limestone and topped with a handsome barrel-tile roof. Tilton commissioned Salvatore Lascari, an accomplished muralist and portrait painter from New York, to design a mosaic facade for the main entrance loggia. The brilliantly colored glass tesserae were assembled in Venice, Italy, and installed in Manchester during the summer of 1930. The three panels illustrate "Pagan art" (left), "Christian art" (right), and "The Fountain of Inspiration" (center).

Tilton also commissioned Salvatore Lascari to embellish the court area. The artist created a mosaic floor of black and white marble, with the signs of the zodiac embedded in a circular pattern in the center of the room. For the court as a whole he developed a lively color scheme to complement the marble staircase and enliven the open arcades. Inspired by the Italian Renaissance and influenced by prevailing Beaux-Arts tastes, Lascari painted geometric motifs highlighted in gold leaf on the court ceiling. He adorned the first-floor entryways with colorful bas-relief floral medallions in brilliant reds, greens, and blues, with a painted meandering vine motif on the ceiling vaults. He accented the capitals of the modified Ionic columns in the arcades

FRANK A. KELLY

Fig. 2   South entrance of the Currier in 1954, decorated with flags to
celebrate the Scandinavian exhibition.

with color and inscribed the names of famous artists in gold
leaf on the dark blue-green entablature.

The Currier's grounds were landscaped with an oblong
reflecting pool and stone and concrete terraces, reminiscent of
a classical Renaissance garden. Several large pines and hemlocks
that had once shaded the old mansion were retained to maintain
a distinctively New England contour to the grounds.

The original building of The Currier Gallery of Art is
listed on the National Register of Historic Places.

ATTRIBUTED TO EDWARD T. KNOWLTON, HUSBAND OF THE DIRECTOR

Fig. 3   Second floor arcade in 1930, now the tapestry gallery.

EARLY PROGRAMMING

The Currier Gallery of Art building was not completed until
1929, but museum programming actually started some years
before. In 1921 the trustees began sponsoring entertainments
and educational programs at the Manchester Institute of Arts
and Sciences, under the auspices of The Currier Gallery of Art.
The first such event was a lecture entitled *The Life of St. Francis
of Assisi,* which was illustrated with colored stereopticon views
of the frescoes of thirteenth-century Italian painter, Giotto.

RX189 24- 1-24-95-.gift Currier Gallery of Art $5.00 est.

These programs would continue each year until 1948 and would include art and travel lectures, as well as dance, theater and musical productions, and films.

THE TRUSTEES

The Currier Gallery of Art has profited from the stewardship of a distinguished board of trustees. Each trustee has brought tireless dedication and impressive talents to the Currier. The appointments of the museum's original ten trustees were approved by the probate court in 1917 and 1918. They were: Albert O. Brown, Frank P. Carpenter, Arthur M. Heard, Benjamin A. Kimball, Cyrus H. Little, Charles H. Manning, Walter M. Parker, Robert J. Peaslee, Frank W. Sargeant, and Herman F. Straw.

Prominent in the banking industry were Arthur M. Heard and Walter M. Parker. Albert O. Brown, a banker and lawyer, would become governor of the state in 1921. Another banker, Benjamin A. Kimball, was also a railway official in his native Concord. Early trustee Cyrus H. Little was one of the most respected attorneys in Manchester.

Two of the original trustees, Charles H. Manning and Herman F. Straw, were associated with the Amoskeag Manufacturing Company. Manning was an inventor and former chief engineer and general superintendent of the company. Herman F. Straw was the company's second agent and son of its engineer and first agent, Ezekiel A. Straw. Ezekiel Straw was the first president of the New Hampshire Fire Insurance Company, and served as governor of the state. Herman Straw's son, H. Ellis Straw, a banker, would become a trustee of the Currier in 1928.

Three of the original trustees would serve as presidents of the board: Robert J. Peaslee, Frank P. Carpenter, and Frank W. Sargeant. Judge Peaslee was elected as the first president, serving from 1918 to 1936. His able guidance helped transform The Currier Gallery of Art from an idea into a reality. After the museum was opened, he worked closely with director Maud Briggs Knowlton in shaping its early programs. Peaslee was chief justice of the New Hampshire Supreme Court and a law lecturer at Dartmouth College and Boston University.

His successor was Frank P. Carpenter, a prosperous merchant, manufacturer and banker. Carpenter is remembered as Manchester's greatest philanthropist; at his death in 1938 the city's flags were flown at half-staff. Among his many benefactions are the buildings for the city's public library and for the Manchester Historic Association. In 1927, he gave Dartmouth College the funds to construct the college's first building dedicated to the arts, Carpenter Hall. A trustee since 1918, Carpenter served as president for only a short time, from 1937 until his death in 1938.

Carpenter's daughter, Mary, married Charles B. Manning, the son of trustee Charles H. Manning. Mrs. Manning became a trustee of the Currier in 1937. She devoted her life to community service, and followed in her father's footsteps as a philanthropist. She provided financial support to a number of organizations, including a generous bequest to the Currier upon her death in 1965. Her daughter is trustee emerita Mrs. Priscilla M. Sullivan, widow of John L. Sullivan, Secretary of the Navy under President Truman.

The third board president, Frank W. Sargeant, was the president of the New Hampshire Fire Insurance Company from 1905 to 1938. He maintained several business and civic interests in Manchester, and was vice president of the Manchester Historic Association. Sargeant, who served as president from 1939 to 1947, worked with director Maud Briggs Knowlton and her successor, Gordon M. Smith.

The Currier's connection with the banking, insurance and

industrial interests in the city was maintained with the appointment of Norwin S. Bean as trustee in 1928. Bean held positions with the Manchester Savings Bank, the New Hampshire Fire Insurance Company, and Amoskeag Industries, Inc., a company founded after the closing of the Amoskeag Manufacturing Company in 1935. His father was Nehemiah S. Bean, an inventor who had designed the first of the world-famous Amoskeag steam engines built in Manchester. Bean and his wife Elizabeth founded the Norwin S. and Elizabeth N. Bean Foundation, which would later support many civic projects in Manchester, including programs at the Currier.

The fourth president of the trustees was Peter Woodbury, who, like Judge Peaslee, was prominent in the field of law. Judge Woodbury, appointed as a trustee in 1939, was the first president who had not been one of the original trustees. He was associate justice of the New Hampshire Superior and Supreme Courts, and a justice on the United States Court of Appeals. Active in several educational and civic organizations, Judge Woodbury was president of the board of trustees of the Elliot Hospital in Manchester. He was board president from 1947 to 1969, working with directors Gordon M. Smith, Charles E. Buckley, William Hutton and David S. Brooke.

Woodbury's successor was Raymond H. Daniels, president for many years of S.A. Felton & Son Co., a manufacturing firm in Manchester. He volunteered his time generously to a number of public service organizations, including the YMCA, where he served as president of the board of directors. Daniels was president from 1969 to 1976, working with director Davis S. Brooke. In 1974 the Hillsborough County Superior Court granted a petition filed by Daniels and his fellow trustees to increase the size of the board from ten to twelve members. The court decree permitted the appointment of two additional trustees in 1975, Dr. Sylvio L. Dupuis and Mrs. Peter S. Freedman.

The current president is Kimon S. Zachos, a prominent attorney with directorships in several corporations in the state. In 1965 he was chosen as a White House Fellow, spending a year in the office of attorney general Nicholas Katzenbach. His civic activities have included trusteeships with the Manchester YMCA, New Hampshire College in Manchester, and Havenwood Retirement Community in Concord. He was a member of the New Hampshire House of Representatives from 1969 to 1974, where he was deputy speaker in 1973–1974. He was a director and later chairman of the New Hampshire Charitable Fund. Zachos' activism in support of the Currier has resulted in many gains for the museum, including the three-million-dollar building addition completed in 1982. He has been president since 1976, working with directors David S. Brooke, Robert M. Doty, and Marilyn F. Hoffman.

Serving with president Zachos today are six other trustees who have been on the board for more than 15 years, and who have contributed substantially to the museum's success: Mrs. Peter S. (Elenore) Freedman; Henry M. Fuller; Mrs. Warren R. (Constance) Hedden III; Mrs. Norman F. (Anne) Milne, Jr.; John H. Morison; and Davis P. Thurber. Three former trustees are now honored as trustees emeriti: Raymond H. Daniels; Mrs. Lawrence W. (Mary) Shirley; and Mrs. John L. (Priscilla) Sullivan.

THE DIRECTORSHIP OF MAUD BRIGGS KNOWLTON 1929 - 1946

As the museum gradually came into being as a physical entity, the trustees began their search for the first director. The ideal candidate would be knowledgeable in art, a respected educator, and would possess an appreciation for the social and demographic

COLLECTION, MANCHESTER INSTITUTE OF ARTS AND SCIENCES

Fig. 4   Maud Briggs Knowlton, the first director, photographed c. 1929.

make-up of the community, as well as a personal dedication to promoting the arts in the life of the city. As it turned out, this person was close at hand. In May 1929 the trustees selected as the first director of The Currier Gallery of Art one of their own, Maud Briggs Knowlton.

Knowlton was an accomplished artist and craftswoman who had apprenticed with noted teachers in Boston, New York, Italy and Holland, and had studied art history at the Museum of Fine Arts, Boston. Her credentials included more than twenty-five years as an instructor at the Manchester Institute of Arts and Sciences. Knowlton's firm orientation in the arts and her self-confidence and grace proved assets for working in the male-dominated museum field. She would effectively shape the new institution into a vital community resource and a respected entity within the greater art world. The origins for much of the Currier's current programming can be found in her early projects.

In 1929 Manchester was an industrial city with an economically and ethnically mixed population of approximately 77,000 citizens. Just twenty days after the Currier's gala opening party the New York Stock Exchange collapsed, triggering events which led to the Great Depression and years of economic hardship for the country. By 1929 Manchester was already suffering through the decline of the textile industry in the Northeast, and in 1935 the city would face the closing of its largest industry, the Amoskeag Manufacturing Company.

Knowlton was fervent in her belief that the Currier could have a positive influence on anyone who came in contact with it. The vital role that the museum could play during times of difficulty was of foremost importance to her. Fortunately, the Currier would be able to operate without interruption in the years ahead due to the prudent management of its endowment by the trustees.

At first, Knowlton had little more than empty galleries to work with, as the museum's collection was very small. She filled the rooms with loan exhibitions from other museums, from artists' organizations, private collectors and commercial galleries in Boston, New York, Washington, Philadelphia and other cities. The museum's schedule, almost 40 exhibitions a year, included work in all media, in all styles and from many different countries.

One of the outstanding circulating exhibitions in the early years was the 1931 showing of bronze sculpture by the French master, Auguste Rodin. Another event of importance was the 1938 summer exhibition of figure and animal sculpture by American artist Anna Hyatt Huntington. The show filled almost the entire museum, while Huntington's heroic outdoor monuments were installed on the museum grounds. As a local newspaper described:

> The main court of the gallery, displays a fine grouping of a large portion of the wild animal studies. There are tigers, lions, cranes, hawks, monkeys, elephants, and a host of others, literally converted from their natural positions and actions into the mediums of bronze and aluminum. The effect of the arrangement is greatly enhanced by a background of palms and ferns, creating an almost natural habitat for the animals represented.[5]

The exuberant display of the Huntington show was representative of Knowlton's outlook toward exhibition installation. As she described:

> There is always a look on faces [of the museum visitors] as though they were on a voyage of discovery. . . . So it follows that installation of exhibits play [sic] no small part

in the educational value to the public. The reason that many art museums are not popular is because, what is housed within their walls, is not understood and there is no easy way for the public to acquire elementary knowledge of the objects at which they gaze in wonderment.[6]

Knowlton strove to make each display as inviting and as instructional as possible. Art objects often were shown in a period-room setting or other appropriate context. Her exhibition style, which might appear cluttered to the modern eye, was influenced by Victorian and Beaux-Arts tastes. The already profusely decorated court area was further embellished with a variety of live plants in decorative pots—maidenhair ferns, palms and trailing vines.

Knowlton wanted the Currier's audience to become cognizant of current trends in American art. She regularly featured one-man and group shows of works by contemporary American artists. Many of these were traveling exhibitions, but several were organized by the Currier. Among her most significant accomplishments were the seven large invitational shows in the summers of 1934, 1936, and 1938 to 1942. Among the artists represented were some of the most celebrated painters of the early twentieth century, including Reginald Marsh, Grant Wood, Thomas Hart Benton, John Steuart Curry, Andrew Wyeth, N.C. Wyeth and Charles Burchfield.

Knowlton established the Currier's now long-standing tradition of fostering artists who live and work in New England. Several of the circulating exhibitions featured artists from the region, and the 1939 summer invitational focused on artists from Maine, New Hampshire and Vermont. In 1937 the Currier displayed works by members of the MacDowell Colony, the respected artists' retreat in Peterborough, New Hampshire.

During summers, Knowlton and her husband sailed to

the island of Monhegan off the coast of Maine, where they built a north-light studio. She painted watercolors, enjoyed the sea air, and participated in the life of this world-famous art colony. It is there that she became acquainted with a young artist, Andrew Wyeth. Impressed with his work, she invited him to show at the Currier. The result was his first one-man museum show, held in 1939, when he was only twenty-one years old. Wyeth also participated in the Currier's summer invitationals of 1939 to 1942.

The museum maintained three permanent installations: the Colonial Room, which contained early-American decorative arts on loan from local collectors; the Children's Room, in which dolls, miniature furniture, and other objects of interest to young visitors were displayed; and the Currier Memorial Room. Knowlton showed works from the small permanent collection, and continued to display the Currier's collection of plaster casts of historical sculpture. Also, in accordance with museum practices of the day, she occasionally exhibited reproductions of master paintings for educational purposes.

Although it was rumored that Hannah Currier had been quietly collecting art for the new museum during the later years of her life, neither she nor her husband had been connoisseurs of art. Their collection consisted primarily of commissioned portraits of themselves and of other members of the Currier family. When the museum opened in 1929, its permanent collection was made up of these portraits and the approximately one hundred paintings of the Leighton bequest of 1918. It also included the Felix Sauvenet wallpaper given to the museum by Penelope Snow, and a few miscellaneous objects from the Currier estate. Shortly after the opening, Knowlton began to purchase important works of art, including the bronze fountain sculpture in the court, *The Crest of the Wave*, by Harriet Frishmuth, an American artist who had studied under Rodin.

It was Knowlton's challenge first to define the new museum's acquisition policy and then to begin amassing works to form the core of a permanent collection of fine and decorative arts. She stated her philosophy as, "It is very essential that collections be brought together with the greatest care, and whatever is to form a part of a permanent collection . . . should be of outstanding merit."[7] and "One good canvas is worth a whole gallery of undistinguished painting."[8] She and her successors seldom wavered from this concept of acquiring only the best works of art.

In a few bold moves Knowlton set the tone for future collecting at the Currier. One of her first orders of business was to begin a collection of early-American decorative arts. She proceeded according to the trustees' wish to, " . . . strive for a collection of the best examples of early American furniture, particularly those pieces which are characteristic of New England . . . ."[9]

As a major step toward this goal, Knowlton acquired the Howe collection in 1932. This assemblage had filled three rooms in the Hopkinton home of the collector, Mrs. DeWitt Clinton (Katherine B.) Howe. Mrs. Howe (later Mrs. Palmer) was one of few collectors of her day to recognize the importance of early-American decorative arts. Over a twenty-year period of active collecting, she was able to acquire pieces from eighteenth century New England that would later prove to be of extraordinary value. Included in the 1932 purchase were fine examples of furniture, pewter, textiles, and household utensils.

The Currier would make several more purchases from the Howe collection in the next few years. The Howe acquisitions provided the museum with a base on which to build its decorative arts holdings.

In 1935 Knowlton purchased the portrait of *John Greene* by John Singleton Copley. This was an important step in establishing the museum's small, but significant collection of historical American paintings. Knowlton set another precedent with the acquisitions, in 1933, of the portrait of *John Clerk of Eldin* by the Scottish master, Sir Henry Raeburn, and in 1937, of the magnificent fifteenth-century Franco-Flemish tapestry, *The Visit of the Gypsies*. These purchases helped establish the Currier as an important collector of European art. Two later acquisitions confirmed this standing: in 1940, a French polychrome wood sculpture, *Madonna and Child* (c. 1350) by an unknown artist; and in 1945, a *Madonna and Child* (c. 1480) in polychrome terracotta by the Italian sculptor Benedetto da Maiano.

Knowlton firmly believed in the value of collecting art by modern American artists. This opinion was shared by few professionals in the museum field at that time. As she stated:

> We must not lose sight of the fact that if we want to develop a great art in this country, we must encourage it by not only getting the works of our artists before the public, but also by purchasing examples . . . .[10]

To this end, she acquired *The Goldfish Window* by American Impressionist, Childe Hassam. Its purchase was considered of such interest that it was announced in the photogravure section of *The New York Times*. Knowlton acquired the charming portrait of *Mary Ann with Her Basket* by Robert Henri, an artist of the Ash Can School of realist painters. She also acquired the *Portrait of Marchioness Curzon of Kedleston*, John Singer Sargent's last portrait of a woman, painted only three months before his death.

Hundreds of objects were acquired during Knowlton's tenure, many by gift. In 1931 three charcoal drawings by John Singer Sargent were received from the artist's sister, Emily Sargent. The Florence Andrews Todd bequest of 1937 included oil paintings by nineteenth-century French landscape painters Eugène Isabey and Henri-Joseph Harpignies, and a bronze sculpture *The Bronco Buster* by Frederic Remington. In 1940 the widow of Childe Hassam gave the Currier a portfolio of etchings and lithographs by the artist. A donation of major importance was the Richard J. Healey collection of glass, which included 4,000 excellent examples of nineteenth-century American glassmaking. It was bequeathed to the museum in 1942.

On Thursday, October 10, 1929, the day after the museum's formal opening, the Currier welcomed the public for the first time. That day brought the museum its first visit from a school group, woodworking students from a local public school. The students spent two hours studying the colonial-era furniture on display. Student groups of all ages have been a familiar and welcome sight at the Currier ever since.

One of the first purchases of the new museum was a movie projector, and film was used extensively in the early years as an educational medium for both children and adults. Regular programs for children, including gallery tours and art appreciation classes, were established early. The Currier's first art teacher was Mildred Kershaw, who was also an instructor at the Manchester Institute of Arts and Sciences. Her popular story hours were often filled to capacity, and when the weather was cold, the children would cluster around a blazing fire in one of the gallery fireplaces. When Kershaw died in 1935, she was succeeded by Thelma Adams (later Thelma Adams Taggart). Adams was an artist and teacher who had been a student of Kershaw. Adams often animated her story hours with lantern projections of her delightful illustrations.

In 1939, the Currier purchased the large house and lot directly to its north. This stately home, with its dormered mansard roof and massive central tower, had been built in the late 1860s and was originally known as the Kennard Estate.

The building and its carriage house were renovated for use as studio classes and exhibition space for children. When the new children's annex opened for classes in the fall of 1939, the students were asked to contribute three pennies each to defray the cost of art materials. The annex continued operation until the fall of 1943, when the war effort made it necessary to close the school due to a fuel shortage and lack of staffing. It opened again temporarily in the summer of 1945, with Maria Kostyshak (Mrs. Z. Peter Graubart) as instructor.

In addition to the in-museum programs, Knowlton also experimented with an outreach project to local public schools. In 1939 and 1940 her assistant, Marjorie Woodruff, a trained museum educator, conducted classes in the schools. The project met with success, but was discontinued as museum resources became limited at the onset of World War II.

Knowlton promoted the museum through the distribution of a calendar of events called the *Bulletin*, and through publicity in the local press and on the radio. She embraced the public, and welcomed social clubs and other groups into the museum for tours, receptions and programs in the auditorium. She considered the Currier not only a gallery for the display of art, but also a community center. She organized free lectures and movies for adults. Most of these programs related to art, but travelogues and lectures on scientific and other topics were also presented. The Currier was closed on Saturdays, but Knowlton often scheduled events on Sundays to accommodate the working population.

Knowlton established the museum's program of free concerts. The first of these was a performance of the Boston Symphony Trio held on Easter, 1930. This event attracted an audience so large that the latecomers had to sit on the windowsills. Knowlton arranged for additional musical performances, and by 1936 the concert program had developed into a yearly series of musical events including chamber music, solo piano, vocal recitals, and lecture recitals. The court made an intimate and elegant setting for these occasions with the musicians performing in the tapestry gallery. The Currier concert program, which continues to the present day as the Sunday Concert Series, maintains a large and loyal following.

To complete the offerings of the new Currier Gallery of Art, Knowlton arranged for the development of an art library which could be used by museum visitors. Many books were received as gifts or bequests.

In 1938 Knowlton hired a young man, Melvin E. Watts, as the first registrar of the museum. Watts' association with the Currier had started in 1930 when, as a high school freshman, he visited the museum each month as part of his art assignment. He went on to complete a four-year fine arts course at the Manchester Institute of Arts and Sciences and to do graduate work at Harvard University. Watts had no intention of staying at the Currier for any great length of time, as his interest lay in the area of art education, not in museum work. He soon discovered that his aspirations as an educator could be satisfied within the museum context, and that he could use his artistic ability in the installation of exhibitions. Watts later became curator and stayed with the Currier for 43 years, leaving the museum only once to serve in the Navy for 30 months during World War II.

Because of the extraordinary circumstances of the Depression era and then of World War II, Knowlton adapted the Currier's programming to meet special needs. During the 1930s the Currier cooperated with government relief agencies including the Federal Art Project and the Civilian Conservation Corps. The museum presented works generated by participants in these projects, and also hosted two concerts by the Symphony Orchestra of New Hampshire under the auspices of the Works Progress Administration. In 1937 the Currier presented an important traveling exhibition organized by the Resettlement Administration. The show included documentary photographs by Walker Evans, Ben Shahn, Dorothea Lange and others. Their powerful images of poverty in the Depression-era South have become etched in the American conscience.

The country was not yet on its feet when World War II was declared. Knowlton believed that:

> Today, more than at any period in the development of mankind, do we need to uphold and sustain the finer qualities of life in order that we may, when peace is once more a reality, go forward with greater assurance that the whole world will be reconstructed on a foundation of enduring goodwill.[11]

During the War, Knowlton was forced to operate the museum with a reduced staff, as several employees were serving in the armed forces. It became almost impossible to organize exhibitions of contemporary art as many American artists were engaged in the war effort. However, the Currier continued to provide enriching and entertaining programming. The museum presented films and entertainments for children and screened current documentary films for adults. As part of its schedule of changing exhibitions, the Currier presented a number of traveling exhibitions of war-related photos and illustrations.

In 1943 Knowlton hired an able assistant, John W. Chandler. Chandler was an instructor at the Manchester Institute of Arts and Sciences from 1930–1948. He was educated at Boston University, Harvard and Columbia. He stayed on as assistant to the director until 1952 when he left the Currier to become an instructor of art at Lycoming College in Williamsport, Pennsylvania. He was later named chairman of the college's art department, a position which he held until his retirement in 1970.

Knowlton retired in 1946 but remained an active trustee until her death in 1956. A local author wrote of her in 1939:

When approaching the executive head of a large corporation or institution, a stranger is usually prepared to meet a person stern, or rigid in character, but the visitor to The Currier Gallery of Art finds, instead, a gracious personage in Mrs. Maud Briggs Knowlton. . . . In a serene and intellectual atmosphere congenial to her tastes; surrounded by art treasures of which she is a connoisseur, and in the autumnal glow of a life, rich in its accomplishments, she presides with quiet efficiency over The Currier Gallery of Art, raised by the will of a scholar, who loved the true and the beautiful. And Mrs. Maud Briggs Knowlton will leave a pleasant imprint, as enduring as the building and the name it bears.[12]

THE DIRECTORSHIP OF
GORDON M. SMITH
1946 - 1955

The Currier's second director, Gordon Mackintosh Smith, was an art historian educated at Williams College, Princeton and Harvard. He was an experienced curator who brought new ideas to the Currier, and strove successfully to establish its reputation as one of the best small museums in the country.

When Smith joined the Currier in 1946, one of his major goals was the refinement of the museum's acquisition policy. He focused primarily on expanding the museum's holdings in American and European painting. His policy was to acquire only superlative examples of an artist's work. He wrote in 1952:

The idea we have heard most often is that a small museum should make no attempt to collect important paintings, should not compete, but should realize that it is the little sister of large institutions, and as such should be grateful for "cast-offs" . . . should be satisfied with comparatively unimportant works. . . . The Currier Gallery of Art . . . has formed an acquisition policy which is quite different from the above. . . . Our long-range objective is a necessarily small, but very choice collection of top-quality paintings, each making a distinct contribution toward an appreciation and understanding of the major movements and periods in history.[13]

Smith persuaded the trustees to loosen the purse strings and to allow him to purchase outstanding works which would move the Currier into the ranks of important American museums. Smith proved to be a discriminating collector, acquiring several masterpieces including *Portrait of a Lady* of c. 1506 by Lorenzo Costa; *Madonna and Child* by the Italian Renaissance master, Pietro Perugino; Dutch master Jacob van Ruisdael's *View of Egmond-on-the-Sea;* and a *Self-Portrait* by the Flemish painter, Jan Gossaert (known as Mabuse).

Perhaps his most brilliant move was the purchase, in 1949, of *The Seine at Bougival* by Claude Monet, an important early landscape by the artist. In the same year he also acquired *Dedham Lock and Mill* by John Constable; Jean-Baptiste Corot's *The Bridge at Grez-sur-Loing;* and, with funds from the Mabel Putney Folsom bequest, *Pietro Capello, Governor of the Venetian Province of Friuli* by Jacopo Robusti (called Tintoretto), the Venetian High Renaissance artist.

One of the highlights of the twentieth-century collection was Pablo Picasso's 1941 *Woman Seated in a Chair,* received in 1950 as an anonymous gift. In the field of American painting, Smith acquired *Moat Mountain, Intervale*, by nineteenth-century Hudson River School artist Albert Bierstadt.

In 1948 the celebrated American painter Charles Sheeler was commissioned to create a work for the Currier's collection. Earlier that year the museum had presented a small exhibition of works by Sheeler. Smith sensed that Sheeler, painter of stark images of the American industrial landscape, would be the ideal artist to create an image of Manchester's millyards for the Currier's collection. At Smith's invitation, Sheeler arrived that summer in Manchester, bringing his wife and two dogs. The artist spent three productive weeks photographing and sketching the massive mill buildings which had been constructed by the Amoskeag Manufacturing Company. The Currier commissioned the oil painting, later entitled *Amoskeag Canal,* from one of the sketches, and today it is regarded as one of Sheeler's finest works.

The museum's decorative arts collection was strengthened with the acquisition of a c. 1780 maple chest-on-chest and a c. 1750 silver cream pot by Paul Revere, Senior.

Under Smith, the number of exhibitions organized by the Currier increased, and the museum's cooperation with other institutions and with important lenders was expanded. Assisting in the organization and installation of exhibitions was Melvin E. Watts, who was named as the Currier's first curator in 1946.

One of the most notable exhibitions in the Currier's history was the 1949 *Monet and the Beginnings of Impressionism,* organized as part of the museum's twentieth anniversary celebration. The museum's newly acquired Monet landscape provided the centerpiece of the exhibition which included additional works by Monet, as well as paintings by Cézanne, Constable, Corot, Courbet, Degas, Manet, Pissarro and Renoir.

Smith re-established the Currier's contact with Andrew Wyeth, who by this time had become one of America's most famous artists. In 1950 the museum purchased his tempera painting, *Spindrift.* In 1951 in cooperation with the William A. Farnsworth Library and Art Museum of Rockland, Maine, the Currier organized the most comprehensive exhibition of Wyeth's work yet assembled. Melvin Watts worked with Andrew Wyeth and his wife Betsy on both the Manchester and Rockland installations. Wyeth was successful in encouraging hesitant collectors to part with their paintings during the months of the show and, as a result, the exhibition contained almost every important tempera Wyeth had produced to that date, as well as a fine group of watercolors and drawings.

In 1947, the museum presented a memorial exhibition of painter Alexander James (1890–1946). James, who made his home in Dublin and Richmond, New Hampshire, was the son of the American philosopher William James and a nephew of the novelist Henry James. The exhibition traveled to the Museum of Fine Arts, Boston, and the Corcoran Gallery of Art, Washington. The paintings of Paul Sample, then artist-in-residence at Dartmouth College, were shown in 1948, and in 1953 the Currier organized an exhibition of the paintings of John Hatch, an instructor of art at the University of New Hampshire.

Smith took an interest in the New Hampshire Art Association, a state-wide group of artists and patrons organized in 1940. He invited the Association to hold its first juried show at the Currier in 1947, an event which continues to be repeated annually. Under Smith, the museum also fostered interest in New Hampshire craftspeople, presenting in 1948 an exhibition of ceramics by Edwin and Mary Scheier, instructors at the University and members of the League of New Hampshire Arts and Crafts (later the League of New Hampshire Craftsmen). The museum cooperated with the League, founded in 1932, in presenting the group's first juried show at the Currier in 1950.

Demonstrating an interest in children's art, Smith cooperated with the state department of education under Dr. Alice A. D. Baumgarner in presenting annual exhibitions of work produced by New Hampshire school children. These shows started in 1951 and continued for several years.

During Smith's tenure, the Currier continued to present traveling exhibitions, including the 1947 show of paintings and sculpture by Thomas Eakins; the 1952 exhibition of paintings by the French master Jean-Auguste-Dominique Ingres from the Musée Ingres in Montauban, France; and the 1954 *Design in Scandinavia,* an exhibition of contemporary designs of household objects from Denmark, Finland, Norway and Sweden. Smith served on the American committee of organization for the latter show.

In 1948 Smith turned his attention to the children's annex which had been closed since 1945 and was badly in need of repairs. He hired Gyorgy Kepes, artist, educator, and internationally recognized authority on color and light,[14] as a consultant for the renovation project. Studio spaces were modernized and new lighting was installed. The building was reopened in the fall of 1948 as the home of the newly established Currier Art Center.

During the next ten years, the school provided studio classes for both children and adults, under a succession of distinguished art educators. The Art Center's supervisors during those years were: Louise Mossgraber Cardeiro (1948), Patricia Vance (1949), David Guillaume (1950–1952), Paul A. Dufour (1952–1955), and Joseph Trippetti (1955–1958).

In 1949 Kepes returned to the Currier, now to help modernize the museum interior. He improved the lighting throughout the museum and repainted the galleries. The gallery walls were painted several tones of gray. The particular tone for a wall was chosen scientifically by measuring the amount of light that wall received during the course of a day. The more light, the darker the shade chosen. Occasional walls were painted with carefully chosen primary colors which provided reflected light flattering to the artwork on display.

FRANK A. KELLY

Fig. 5   Director Gordon Smith, right, with Wilhelm Munthe de
Morgenstierne, ambassador of Norway, left, at the opening of
Design in Scandinavia, 1954.

Salvatore Lascari's competent, but not masterful, decor in the museum court now appeared incongruous with contemporary concepts of museum design. His work was either removed or covered over and the court was also painted in shades of gray. Smith removed the potted plants and other paraphernalia from the court and galleries, and boarded up the fireplaces. He then reinstalled the permanent collection in uncluttered arrangements.

The new look contrasted radically with the previous Victorian and Beaux-Arts ambience. The change shocked some local residents, especially coming as it did during the Currier's twentieth anniversary year. But many others found the unadorned clarity of the new to be refreshing. They welcomed the feeling of spaciousness and the contemporary elegance. Any rumblings of discontent eventually faded away.

Smith continued the Currier's relationship with Kepes, organizing a show of his paintings and photographs at the museum in 1951. Kepes again exhibited at the Currier in 1955, along with Italian architect and industrial designer, Gio Ponti, in a show organized by Boston's Institute of Contemporary Art.

The Currier advanced in its role as a social and cultural center. Local clubs, professional organizations, and arts groups regularly made use of the museum's facilities. This included the Manchester Film Society, which promoted the cinema as an art form.

The museum held its first opening reception in May 1947, celebrating the arrival of the Thomas Eakins exhibition circulated by the Philadelphia Museum of Art. The event attracted two hundred guests and was described in a local newspaper, "The gallery, always one of the city's beauty spots, was in festive dress for the occasion with spray bouquets of apple blossoms and quince set in strategic spots."[5] This occasion would prove to be an auspicious beginning to what would become one of Manchester's most enduring social traditions—The Currier Gal-

MANCHESTER EVENING LEADER

Fig. 6   The first exhibition opening party, held in 1947, was a tea to celebrate the Thomas Eakins retrospective. The pourers were former director Maud Briggs Knowlton, left, and Mrs. Charles B. Manning, trustee, right. Among the over 200 guests were, left to right, Mrs. Herbert P. Detjens; Mrs. Wesley E. Barbour; Mrs. Robert Peaslee, widow of the Currier's first president; Mrs. Raymond H. Daniels, wife of a trustee; Ruth W. Higgins, trustee; Mrs. Peter Woodbury, wife of the Currier's board president; Florence C. Derr, trustee; and Mrs. H. Ellis Straw, wife of a trustee.

lery of Art openings. In future years, these events would include everything from black tie galas to Saturday afternoon punch parties for children.

Smith continued with the Sunday programming started under Knowlton and expanded the popular concert series, offering as many as eleven programs of classical music a year. The Currier continued to sponsor entertainments in conjunction with the Manchester Institute of Arts and Sciences. The last program, held in 1948, was a dance concert presented at Manchester's

Practical Arts High School Auditorium (now Central High School).

Under Smith the museum instituted modern curatorial techniques in the management and conservation of its growing collection. The museum expanded its publications program by developing the *Bulletin* into a more extensive and scholarly publication, and by publishing illustrated catalogues for major exhibitions. The Currier improved its library through the addition of standard art reference materials. Smith enhanced the Currier's reputation through his participation in museum professional associations. He was a frequent speaker at social functions, and was in demand as an exhibition juror.

Smith resigned in 1955 to accept the post of director of the Albright Art Gallery (during his tenure renamed the Albright-Knox Art Gallery) in Buffalo, New York. During his distinguished career in Buffalo he oversaw a major expansion project and acquired outstanding works of contemporary art. Smith's last visit to the Currier was in 1964 when he returned to jury the eighteenth annual New Hampshire Art Association show. He retired as director of the Albright-Knox Art Gallery in 1973 and died in 1979.

Elizabeth (Bowser) Smith, Gordon Smith's wife, was an art historian and journalist who assisted her husband both at the Currier and later in Buffalo. She was hired in 1947 to produce the Currier's *Bulletin* and to handle museum publicity. She died in 1959.

THE DIRECTORSHIP OF
CHARLES E. BUCKLEY
1955 - 1964

Charles Edward Buckley was the curator of the Wadsworth Atheneum in Hartford, Connecticut, before coming to the Currier in 1955. He was educated at the School of the Art Institute of Chicago and at Harvard. His approach to the directorship of the Currier effectively blended his considerable scholarly and diplomatic talents. He was successful in bringing to the museum people with widely differing tastes and opinions about art.

Buckley collected with discernment and with courage, as his commitment to the aggressive acquisition of modern American art ran counter to the prevailing opinion of the day. Among the significant modern American paintings he purchased were *The Mill in Spring* by Lyonel Feininger, *Abundance* by Marsden Hartley, *Lancer* by Walt Kuhn, *Cross by the Sea* by Georgia O'Keeffe, and *The Bootleggers* by Edward Hopper. The museum purchased Maurice Prendergast's watercolor, *The Stony Pasture* and received as a gift Winslow Homer's watercolor, *The North Woods (Playing Him)*.

In the area of sculpture Buckley acquired *Seated Bather* by sculptor, Jacques Lipchitz. Buckley also collected historical American works, including the monumental *Indian Summer Morning in the White Mountains*, a painting by nineteenth-century artist Jasper Francis Cropsey, and *Marshfield Meadows* by Martin Johnson Heade.

Buckley strengthened the museum's collection of European painting with a masterwork by sixteenth-century Flemish painter Joos van Cleve, *The Holy Family*. Among the twentieth-century European works he purchased were Henri Matisse's bronze, *Seated Nude*, and the Fauve painting, *The Wounded Clown*, by Georges Rouault. A surrealist painting, *Mira*, by Yves Tanguy was bequeathed by painter Kay Sage, Tanguy's wife. The museum received an important piece of modern sculpture, Sir Jacob Epstein's 1957 bronze, *Kitty III*, as a gift of Dr. Isadore J. and Lucille Zimmerman.

Buckley renewed the museum's early commitment to collecting early-American furniture and other decorative arts, and placed particular emphasis on acquiring pieces with a New Hampshire origin. Assisted by curator Melvin Watts, Buckley assembled, through gift and purchase, a select group of outstanding objects, including a tiger maple chest-on-chest-on-frame and a maple desk attributed to New Hampshire's early cabinetmakers, the Dunlaps, and a magnificent early nineteenth-century tall clock by Levi Hutchins of Concord.

The Currier's holdings in the decorative arts served as the basis for the development of important exhibitions and publications. The museum organized the pioneering 1958 show, *New Hampshire Silver 1775–1825*. Based on research conducted by Charles H. Batchelder of Portsmouth, it was the first attempt to present a cross-section of works by the state's early silversmiths. The culminating effort of Buckley's tenure was the 1964 show, *The Decorative Arts of New Hampshire 1725–1825*. This pioneering survey was organized with the assistance of a volunteer committee of experts. Illustrated catalogues were published for both exhibitions.

The Currier's reputation as a major resource for the scholarship of New England decorative arts was extended through its participation in the Heritage Forum. This series of yearly lectures, seminars and exhibitions on the cultural legacy of the state was started in 1962 through the cooperation of several organizations. Both Buckley and Watts were honored by the Forum for their contributions to the study and preservation of the state's heritage.

Under Buckley the Currier produced important exhibitions that helped forge closer ties with other art institutions. One of these was *Watercolors by Edward Hopper* in 1959, produced in conjunction with the Wadsworth Atheneum and the Museum of Art of the Rhode Island School of Design. This was the first major showing of Hopper's work in New England in a decade. In 1962 the museum worked with the Corcoran Gallery of Art to prepare *John Marin in Retrospect*. After showings in Washington and Manchester, the exhibition traveled to West Berlin under the auspices of the United States Information Agency.

For the museum's thirty-fifth anniversary in 1964 Buckley organized the first full-scale retrospective of American surrealist Peter Blume, which was mounted in cooperation with the Wadsworth Atheneum. The same year the Currier featured *Textiles of Oaxaca,* an exhibition of Mexican textiles assembled by potter Gerry Williams and his wife Julie, working with the Hopkins Center at Dartmouth College.

The museum turned its focus to Manchester's architecture in two exhibitions by photographer and art educator, Gerda Peterich. Peterich had exhibited at the Currier in 1949 and 1952 and would later become associated with the museum as a guest lecturer and contract photographer. In 1960 the museum presented her show entitled *Frank Lloyd Wright in Manchester* in which she documented in black-and-white photography the architecture of two Wright-designed houses. One of these was the home of Dr. Isadore J. and Lucille Zimmerman, completed in 1952. The Zimmermans' home eventually would become part of the museum's collection, and Peterich's work would provide a valuable record of the house and its furnishings in its early years.

Peterich conducted a photographic study of Manchester's Victorian-era architecture which culminated in the 1964 show *The Architecture of Manchester 1840—1900*. Photographs from this exhibition document several important structures which have since been destroyed. Images from both of these shows are preserved in the Currier's collection.

The Currier's association with another photographer, Lotte Jacobi, began in 1959. Jacobi had gained international renown for her portraits of dancers and theatrical figures in 1920s and 1930s Berlin. She immigrated to the United States from Ger-

Fig. 7 Director Charles Buckley with celebrated photographer Lotte Jacobi at her Currier exhibition in 1959.

many in 1935, first settling in New York City. In 1955 she moved to Deering, New Hampshire, where she established a workshop and studio. In 1959 Buckley organized a retrospective of approximately two hundred of her photographs. She exhibited again at the Currier in 1964, where her abstract works called "photogenics" were included as part of the New Hampshire Art Association's twenty-fifth anniversary show. Jacobi became a cherished associate of the Currier, contributing her wisdom and knowledge toward the establishment of the museum's photography collection.

FRANK A. KELLY

Fig. 8   Education director Marian D. Woodruff conducting a tour in
1964 for Ash Street School children; Betsy Herrick, Karen Welch
and James McDowell, left to right.

Like his predecessors, Buckley presented group and one-man shows of regional artists. He took a particular interest in the League of New Hampshire Arts and Crafts, and served as its president from 1957 to 1964. Under his aegis the Currier frequently exhibited works by craftspeople from the region. This patronage helped to elevate the status of craftspeople in the state by creating an awareness of the crafts as branches of the fine arts. Buckley's *Good Design* exhibitions in 1957, 1958 and 1959 presented commercially produced household objects available locally, chosen for their beauty as art objects as well as for their utility.

Buckley organized several distinguished loan exhibitions. In 1960 he created the first major survey of works held in private collections in New Hampshire, *Collecting in the Granite State*. The Currier also presented traveling exhibitions of note. One of these was a spectacular showing in 1960 of Greek historical costumes and embroideries. Financial and volunteer support for the exhibition came from the Greek community. An exhibition organized by the Museum of Modern Art in New York gave the Currier's audience a rare opportunity in 1961 to view portraits executed by twentieth-century masters, including Modigliani, Picasso, Chagall and Matisse.

To foster a greater understanding of art in its many forms, Buckley arranged for lectures and other educational programs for adults, and maintained the Currier's program of free concerts. He established a long-range educational program to reach students in the state's public schools, which was developed under the direction of museum educator Marian Davis Woodruff, who joined the staff in 1962. Woodruff is a graduate of Smith College, with graduate study at the Rhode Island School of Design and New York University, and museum education experience at The Metropolitan Museum of Art in New York, and the Museum of Art, Rhode Island School of Design. Under Buckley she conducted classes in schools, organized tours and workshops for student groups visiting the museum, and loaned slides and study materials to New Hampshire schools.

In early 1958 Buckley and Joseph Trippetti, considering the future of the Currier's museum school, decided to eliminate the adult classes at the Art Center in favor of developing a first-class studio arts program for children, leaving classes for adults to the Manchester Institute of Arts and Sciences. Trippetti left that spring to pursue other interests, and Robert Eshoo was hired to carry out the new program. This was the beginning of more than three decades of model arts education programs for elementary and high school students. In 1960 a new studio for sculpture and ceramics was opened. Under Eshoo, the annual exhibition of work produced by the Art Center's students has become one of the most popular annual events at the museum.

Eshoo is a graduate of the School of the Museum of Fine Arts, Boston, with an advanced degree from Syracuse University. He has exhibited his paintings and sculpture in museums and galleries throughout the country, and his work is represented in important collections. Several Art Center teachers have continued with the institution for more than fifteen years, working under Eshoo. These include Maria Kostyshak Graubart, Betsy Guenther, Jean Pinckney Nelson, and Rosemary Uicker.

In 1958 the president of the trustees, Peter Woodbury, trustee Ruth W. Higgins, and Buckley created the Friends of the Currier Gallery of Art. Over the years many benefits have been developed for members. The funds generated from the program have been used to expand the museum's collection of American art. The first purchase from Friends funds, made in 1958, was *The Wood Sled* by George Henry Durrie, a charming nineteenth-century American landscape. Today over a hundred works have been purchased through the Friends, including examples by Edward Hopper, Robert Indiana, Jacques Lipchitz, Lotte Jacobi, and Alexander Calder, as well as American folk art and decorative arts. Recent purchases have also included European sculpture.

The library, in existence since 1929, was reorganized by Donn Purvis, who served as the Currier's librarian from 1964 until his death in 1972. Purvis updated an almost random collection of books and exhibition catalogues into a professional art reference library. A retired librarian from the Library of Congress, Washington, he contributed the wisdom of a lifelong career to the development of the Currier library.

Buckley strengthened communications and cooperation

between the Currier and other cultural institutions. He lectured frequently throughout the region on a variety of topics. He was an instructor of art history at the Manchester Institute of Arts and Sciences and served as a trustee of the New Hampshire Historical Society.

Buckley left the Currier in 1964 to become the director of the City Art Museum in St. Louis, Missouri (under his aegis, renamed The Saint Louis Art Museum). Following an outstanding career in St. Louis, where he guided the museum through a period of growth in its collections and operations, he retired in 1975. He returned to New Hampshire, where he maintains an informal association with the Currier as a lecturer and consultant. A scholar, writer, and art appraiser, he continues to be active in the field.

THE DIRECTORSHIP OF
WILLIAM HUTTON
1965 - 1968

The museum's fourth director, William Hutton, came to the Currier in 1965 after serving as assistant curator of The Toledo Museum of Art in Ohio. An art scholar, he worked to broaden the museum's collections in all areas. Among his acquisitions was *Crucifixion* by the sixteenth-century Spanish painter known as the Astorga Master. He enhanced the museum's American painting collection with the purchase of Charles Burchfield's watercolor *November Sunset*. A painting by Marsden Hartley, *Raptus,* one of the earliest American abstract paintings, was given, and two early nineteenth-century portraits by William Jennys were purchased through Friends funds.

During Hutton's tenure, the Currier acquired notable examples of decorative arts including a c. 1780 mahogany desk built by Major Benjamin Frothingham of Charlestown, Mas-

SUDHALTER, MANCHESTER UNION LEADER

Fig. 9   Director William Hutton, right, on the first Friends' trip in 1967
with, left to right, Marjorie O'Connell, Miriam Sawyer, first row;
Margaret Woodbury with her husband, trustee president Judge
Peter Woodbury, second row; Adelaide Dodge and Lois Booth,
third row.

sachusetts. The desk was a bequest of Mrs. Norwin S. Bean,
and had belonged to her family for several generations. Hutton
arranged for the evaluation of the physical condition of the
museum's furniture collection and initiated a program of
conservation.

The major exhibition organized by the Currier under Hutton was that of works by Edwin Scheier, which included 25
years of ceramics, textiles, prints and drawings. The 1966 show,
which traveled to the Hopkins Center Galleries at Dartmouth
College, was the largest and most inclusive assemblage of
Scheier's work to that date.

Hutton arranged for special projects such as the 1967–1968 series of lectures entitled *Prelude to Progress*, held at the museum and arranged in conjunction with the Manchester Historic Association, talks which increased awareness of urban planning and historic preservation issues in Manchester. Hutton enhanced the Friends benefits by establishing art tours. The first tour, a bus trip to Boston's Museum of Fine Arts, took place in 1967.

After leaving the Currier in 1968, Hutton became a researcher in the department of ceramics at the Victoria and Albert Museum in London. He left there in 1971 to accept the position of senior curator at The Toledo Museum of Art, one of the top curatorial posts in the country, where he remains today.

THE DIRECTORSHIP OF DAVID S. BROOKE 1968 - 1977

David Stopford Brooke, a Harvard-educated Englishman, was the chief curator at the Art Gallery of Ontario in Toronto, Canada, before coming to Manchester in 1968. His energetic leadership broadened the Currier's outlook in all areas. He expressed his view of the Currier as follows:

> Did he [Moody Currier] think of it [The Currier Gallery of Art] as a mausoleum in which one could admire the masters and pay one's respects to the dead? I doubt it; rather as a place to stretch the imagination, to increase one's perception of other people and their surroundings, to teach certain values, and above all to delight.[16]

Brooke's tenure occurred during a time when Manchester was experiencing a revitalization of the arts. The city's

Vaudeville-era theatre, the Palace, was undergoing restoration, and there was a general re-awakening of interest in the performing and visual arts in the city. Brooke was an active participant in this revival, hosting meetings of cultural organizations in the museum, and establishing a reputation as one of the area's most popular speakers on the arts.

Brooke strove to give the museum a more informal and approachable image. He experimented with exhibition programming with the goal of entertaining as well as enlightening. His dramatic flair was apparent in such shows as *Moody Currier's Marvelous Menagerie* in 1969, which featured images of animals in painting and sculpture. This was the first in a series of holiday-season shows for families that included *United Hats of America*, where visitors could participate by trying on a variety of headgear. Another exhibition in this spirit was a traveling production called *Video Maze* which featured closed-circuit electronic "sculpture" with which the visitor could interact.

Under Brooke the Currier's ties with area schools were strengthened, and the museum arranged for puppet shows and other entertainments to bring families into the galleries. Brooke promoted the cinema as a viable art form through themed film series; and with Elinore Adams' help, he brought nationally acclaimed musicians to the museum's concert series. To the traditional concert fare of classical chamber music they added folk music, "new music" and electronic music. A program in this last category included the 1970 lecture-demonstration by Robert Moog with his famous Moog Synthesizer.

Brooke worked to strengthen the Currier's collections, acquiring significant works of American contemporary art. A grant from the National Endowment for the Arts with matching funds allowed for the purchase, in 1973, of several contemporary works including *Dream Houses XXXIII*, by sculptor Louise Nevelson. Another notable contemporary acquisition was Jules Olitski's abstract painting, *Shoot*, purchased with help from the Friends funds and an NEA grant.

The director's British background gave him a particular affinity for European art. He purchased three of the Currier's treasures: *The Banquet of Antony and Cleopatra* by the seventeenth-century Dutch painter, Jan de Bray; a dramatic French marine painting from the eighteenth century, *The Storm*, by Claude Joseph Vernet; and *Martyrdom of St. Bartholomew*, a Baroque work by seventeenth-century Italian Mattia Preti. An important gift was a pastel by Edgar Degas, *Dancers*.

Through Friends funds Brooke acquired a c. 1810 secretary desk, and the decorative arts collection was further enhanced with major gifts. These included the Murray Collection of Glass. This assemblage of nearly four hundred pieces of fine European and American glass includes many rare examples of Victorian, Art Nouveau and Classical styles. The collection had been assembled by Mrs. Albert C. (Sophie) Murray of Temple, New Hampshire, and was given to the museum after her death by her husband and his second wife Priscilla. The museum also received a fine group of British pewter and a c. 1830 Levi Hutchins shelf clock with reverse-painted glass. Through museum and gift funds, the Currier acquired the charming folk art portrait of *Emily Moulton* by Samuel Miller. Brooke also increased holdings in the graphic arts with a group of nineteenth-century lithographic posters purchased in 1974.

The Currier's presentation of groundbreaking exhibitions in the decorative arts continued. *Pewter in America 1650–1900* was organized in 1968 by curator Melvin Watts. Its counterpart, *British Pewter 1600–1850,* was mounted in 1974 with the assistance of pewter collectors in the United States and Great Britain. The Currier's 1970 show, *The Dunlaps and Their Furniture*, featured furniture created by members of New Hampshire's Dunlap family of cabinetmakers. The exhibition was

Fig. 10   Director David Brooke in 1974 discusses one of his most important acquisitions, *The Banquet of Antony and Cleopatra* by Jan de
Bray, purchased in 1969.

organized by Charles S. Parsons, a dedicated researcher of New Hampshire decorative arts. The catalogues for these three projects have become important reference works for scholars.

One of the most impressive of the Currier's exhibitions was that of nineteenth-century American paintings from the collection of Currier trustee, Henry Melville Fuller. Included in the 1971 exhibition were 60 paintings of landscape, genre and still life subjects. Later, Fuller established a fund for the purchase of nineteenth-century American art, which continues to support the acquisition of outstanding works. He has also given paintings from his collection to the museum.

The 1975 show *Amoskeag: A Sense of Place, A Way of Life* was an unprecedented success. The result of a six-year historical and archaeological study of Manchester's millyard conducted by architectural photographer Randolph Langenbach,[17] the installation featured mural-size photographs of the millyard, workers' housing and artifacts from the mills. Visitors to the exhibition listened to taped interviews of former millworkers, assembled as part of an oral history project directed by historian Tamara Hareven.

In 1968 the Currier presented a major reinstallation of its glass collection, following a survey of its holdings conducted by Lowell Innes. Innes, one of the country's foremost authorities on American glass, would continue to work with Brooke to organize the 1969 show, *Nineteenth Century Glass: Plain and Fancy*, and the 1970 show, *Early Glass from New Hampshire Factories*. Innes, who wrote extensively on the Currier glass collection for the *Bulletin* and other publications, was named honorary curator of glass in 1969, and continued as a consultant with the Currier until his death in 1985.

Brooke renewed the Currier's relationship with photographer Lotte Jacobi. She was named honorary curator of photography in 1971 and worked as a consultant on several exhibitions, including shows on photographers Paul Strand and William Manahan. She also provided advice on acquisitions of photographs. In 1974 the Currier mounted *A Photographer's Photographs*, which presented Jacobi's collection of works by other photographers. In future years, Jacobi would support the museum as a patron, giving her own photographs and works from her collection to the museum. Later, her son and daughter-in-law, Mr. and Mrs. John Hunter, also contributed extensively to the permanent collection.

Volunteers had always been important to the success of the Currier since the opening night in 1929 when volunteer ushers greeted the museum's first visitors. During Brooke's tenure, volunteer committees were organized, and in 1972 the Currier began programs to familiarize art teachers in the state with the collection and to train volunteer tour docents. These programs were supervised by education director Marian Woodruff.

In 1976 the trustees established the advisory council to assist them and the museum director in fundraising activities, to encourage gifts to the collection, and to help the museum reach a larger audience. Former director Charles E. Buckley became the first chairperson, serving until October 1980. He was succeeded by Mrs. Saul Greenspan, who served until 1984. She was followed by Mrs. John A. Graf (1985–1987) and Mrs. Douglas Wheeler (1988–to present).

In 1970 Mrs. Ada L. Clark retired. She had served as the Currier's bookkeeper for over 40 years, working for the treasurer of the board of trustees from her office at the Amoskeag National Bank. She helped manage the museum's financial activities under five directors, starting in the early days with Maud Briggs Knowlton.

In 1972, after the death of Donn Purvis, Brooke appointed Maria Kostyshak Graubart as the museum's new librarian. Graubart is an artist and art educator who has served in the Manchester school system, at the Currier Art Center and especially at the Manchester Institute of Arts and Sciences, where she taught drawing and painting and served as assistant and then acting director. She is also an art librarian with experience at the Manchester City Library. Under her stewardship the library has grown to over seven thousand volumes, and serves museum staff, volunteers, scholars and students.

In 1977 Brooke resigned to accept the position of director of the Sterling and Francine Clark Art Institute in Williamstown, Massachusetts, where he continues to serve.

The Directorship of Robert M. Doty 1977 - 1987

In 1977, Robert McIntyre Doty came to the Currier from his post as director of the Akron Art Institute (now the Akron Art Museum) in Ohio. He was educated at Harvard University and the University of Rochester in Rochester, New York. Specializing in contemporary art, folk art and photography, he held administrative and curatorial positions at several museums including five years as curator of the Whitney Museum of American Art in New York.

Doty brought recognition to the Currier through excellence in exhibitions and publications. He also successfully guided the museum through a major fundraising and building project.

Doty organized and curated retrospectives of important contemporary artists and circulated these shows to other institutions. Among the artists were Will Barnet, Tom Blackwell, Jane Freilicher and Neil Welliver. Doty also focused attention on regional artists with the 1988 juried show *New England Now:*

Contemporary Art from Six States, organized with five other New England art institutions. A biennial new talent show, established in 1987, *New Artists/The Gloria Wilcher Memorial Exhibition*, was the first in a series of partially endowed exhibitions made possible by a gift from Abrasha and Lena Wilcher and their family in memory of their daughter.

The Currier's exhibition program continued to provide new perspectives on American decorative arts. Curator Melvin Watts organized the 1979 show *Eagles, Urns and Columns: Decorative Arts of the Federal Period*, which outlined the development of American motifs in furniture, silver, glass and architecture during this period. This was Watts' largest and most important exhibition, the crowning accomplishment of his long career. In 1980 the Currier presented selections of nineteenth-century American toys from the collection of Bernard Barenholtz, a noted toy designer and collector of folk art and antique toys. The Currier hosted two exhibitions on historical themes, both curated by the Dublin Seminar for New England Folk Life: in 1979, *The New England Meeting House and Church: 1630–1850*; and in 1980, *New England Prospect: Maps, Place Names, and the Historical Landscape*. An important exhibition of decorative and fine arts was *Heirlooms, Historical Art and Decorative Arts from New Hampshire Collectors*, organized by curator Marilyn F. Hoffman in 1985. Returning to an emphasis on contemporary crafts, the Currier hosted *American Crafts '81*, a national juried all-media craft exhibition organized by the League of New Hampshire Craftsmen in celebration of its fiftieth anniversary.

Under Doty a number of intimate photography exhibitions were organized, developing the Currier's reputation as a resource for the study of this medium. Contemporary photographers were featured, as well as historical surveys, such as *The Photo-Secession/ The Golden Age of Pictorial Photography in America* in 1983, an exhibition of works by Alfred Stieglitz and his students. Selected

Fig. 11 Curator Melvin E. Watts worked for over 43 years with the first six directors and is an expert on New England decorative arts. Photographed in 1981 at his retirement.

photographs and prints from Lotte Jacobi's eclectic private collection were shown in 1982. The museum presented a one-woman show of her work in 1984 and in 1986 exhibited a newly acquired collection of 50 of her theatre and dance photographs.

Several exhibitions during Doty's tenure focused on particular cultural outlooks. Among these were the 1979 showing of the works of French-Canadian sculptor, Alfred Laliberté, and in 1980, an exhibition of sculpture by a Franco-American artist, Lucien Gosselin, both presented in conjunction with local Franco-American organizations. In 1985 Doty brought together, in cooperation with Shaker Village, Inc., *The Canterbury Shakers*. The show revealed a portrait of life in the Shaker community of Canterbury, New Hampshire, through photographs and examples of Shaker furniture.

Calder's Universe, a major traveling exhibition organized by the Whitney Museum of American Art, was presented in 1979. It was the only New England showing of the exhibition, and it broke all previous attendance records. The spectacular Minnesota Museum of Art exhibition, *Paul Manship: Changing Taste in America*, was mounted in 1986 in the museum's new wings, surveying the career of this New York art deco sculptor who summered in Cornish, New Hampshire.

Under Doty the museum's holdings were enlarged in all categories. Many purchases were aided by grants and private gifts of purchase funds. Among the contemporary works brought into the collection were paintings by Tom Blackwell, Richard Estes, Jane Freilicher, Alex Katz, and Neil Welliver. In 1987 the museum acquired an eighteenth-century Portsmouth side chair by John Gaines III, a purchase made possible through funds contributed by individuals and corporations. In 1983 the Currier purchased the Alexander Calder mobile, *Petit Disque Jaune (Little Yellow Disk)* in honor of the Friends' twenty-fifth anniversary. Contributions came from Friends who had been members since 1958 and other donors.

A William Zorach painting, *Plowing the Fields, New Hampshire* was purchased by a group of generous donors and Friends funds. The imposing *Still Life with Fruit and Champagne* by nineteenth-century German-American painter Severin Roesen was purchased in 1984 through funds provided by trustee Henry Melville Fuller. In the same year Fuller gave the William Holbrook Beard painting, *Susanna and the Elders*. Among the other works that came into the collection by gift were *The Black Hat* by Lilla Cabot Perry; portraits of *Abraham Sleight* and *Ruth Roe Sleight* by Ammi Phillips, a master of nineteenth-century folk painting; and the *Portrait of Master Otis Barton and his Grandfather*, painted by William Merritt Chase in 1903.

Other gifts included the important assemblage of 144 prints by Western and Japanese artists from Stephen C. Sideris and his family; lithographs by Thomas Hart Benton received in memory of Lily Schnur Kurtz; prints and paintings given by A. Aladar Marberger including works by Alex Katz, Jane Freilicher, Sylvia Mangold and John Button; and a group of small sculptures from Joseph L. Desjardins. The museum's holdings in late nineteenth-century glass were reinforced with the addition of the Elisha and Doris Camp Collection of Glass, given by the collectors. A portrait by Thomas Eakins, *Miss Florence Einstein*, painted in 1905, was purchased through the Henry Melville Fuller Fund and museum funds.

During this period the Currier purchased the bronze sculptures *Walking Woman* by Gaston Lachaise and *Hephaestus III* by Dimitri Hadzi through the generosity of Isadore and Lucille Zimmerman. The Currier received Andrew Wyeth's study for the painting *Spindrift* from the estate of former director Gordon M. Smith. The Currier's photography holdings benefitted from gifts in 1982 and 1984 from Vincent Vallarino and his mother, Edith. The Vallarino Collection, totalling over one hundred photographs and portfolios, represents the entire history of photography.

The popularization of the museum continued. The Currier had experimented since the 1940s with evening hours, and in 1978 Doty instituted regular Thursday night hours. The museum scheduled lectures and other events during this time. The Thursday film series, developed in 1978 by director of education Marian Woodruff, quickly became a standard offering. Through these themed series, the Currier has presented a wide variety of films including Hollywood classics, masterpieces from other countries, and the best work of documentary and independent filmmakers and animation studios, including New Hampshire premieres. Talks by filmmakers and film scholars have frequently accompanied the spring film festival.

The education department established *Hidden Treasure Day* in 1978, a day for participants to receive free appraisals on glass, jewelry, paintings and other "objets d'art." The Friends' travel program and concert series had been developed since Hutton's directorship by Elinore Adams. Virginia H. Eshoo took the reins in 1978, expanding the Friends' educational travel program to include additional destinations both inside and outside of New England, and since 1984, European art tours. Jazz offerings were added to the Sunday Concert Series, and the concert program received an important addition in 1985, a new Steinway concert grand piano. Dr. David G. Stahl, longtime advisor to the museum's concert program, helped select a piano which would suit the acoustics and concert needs of the museum. The next year the Currier presented an evening subscription series, *Andrew Rangell Plays Beethoven*, to rave reviews.

The need for volunteer services continued to grow. In 1979 over 85 volunteers worked on various aspects of the *Calder's Universe* show and on other programs. In 1982, under the direction of Marian Woodruff, the volunteer effort was organized into The Currier Gallery Guild of Volunteers. The Guild has thrived under the extraordinary leadership provided by chairpersons Polly Thorner (1982–1983), Helen D. Rosenberg (1984–1985), H. Frances Gordon (1986–1987), Frances P. Nelson (1988–1989) and Patricia K. Dastin (1990–1991). In its first year, the Guild contributed 2,000 hours of work to the museum. In 1989 this figure reached over 10,000 hours. The Guild regularly provides docents for groups visiting the museum, staffs the information and sales desk, and assists in all departments. The Guild organizes special events, including the 1987 dinner dance and benefit auction, the *Fête du Musée*. The funds raised from the *Fête* were contributed toward the purchase of a glass bench sculpture by Howard Ben Tré, installed in 1989. Also in 1989, the Guild organized special events celebrating the museum's sixtieth anniversary.

In 1981 the Currier bid farewell to its first curator, Melvin E. Watts. He had been on the staff of the museum since 1938, and had served as curator since 1946. During his long tenure, Watts' sensitive and creative approach to exhibition design was always evident. His appreciation and knowledge of the art and cultural heritage of New England is monumental. He is particularly well versed in the region's decorative arts and, through his contributions, the museum's holdings in this area gained prominence. His gallery talks and lectures over the years revealed a spirited sense of history and aesthetics, as did his writings. In 1982, Watts was named curator emeritus, and he continues to serve as a consultant to the museum.

In 1980 Philip D. Zimmerman, who had been instrumental in organizing the 1979 *Meeting House* show as the associate director of the Dublin Seminar and who co-authored the text of the accompanying book, became the Currier's associate curator. He was named the museum's second curator in 1981. Zimmerman, a specialist in American decorative arts, was educated at Yale University, the University of Delaware, and Boston University. He resigned in 1983 to accept the position of executive director of The Historical Society of York County in York, Pennsylvania. He remained there until December 1986, when he was named to his current position as senior curator of the Henry Francis du Pont Wintherthur Museum in Delaware.

The Currier's third curator, Marilyn F. Hoffman, joined the staff in 1984 after a ten-year tenure as the director of the Brockton Art Museum/Fuller Memorial in Massachusetts (now the Fuller Art Museum). She received her undergraduate and

BOB RAICHE

Fig. 12 In 1980 trustee president Kimon S. Zachos signed the contract with the architectural firm of Hardy Holzman Pfeiffer for the museum's new wings. Present were, seated left to right, Raymond G. Cote, president of Harvey Construction Company, Inc; Hugh M. Hardy, project architect; Kimon S. Zachos; Mrs. Warren R. (Constance) Hedden III, trustee; and standing, left to right, trustees Davis P. Thurber, James W. Griswold, Mrs. Norman F. (Anne) Milne; museum director Robert M. Doty; and trustee Dr. Sylvio L. Dupuis.

graduate degrees from Brown University and had worked at three larger museums. Among the exhibitions she organized under Doty was *Marguerite and William Zorach: The Cubist Years 1915–1918*. This 1987 show and its accompanying catalogue edited by Hoffman highlighted the paintings produced by the Zorachs in New Hampshire. Extensive conservation of the collections of works on paper and textiles was undertaken under Hoffman. She was named the Currier's seventh director in 1988.

In 1979 Doty published the Currier's first *Handbook of the Collection*, which provided a much-needed resource to scholars and others in the United States and Europe. He wrote many distinguished monographs during his career, most under the aegis of the Currier.

Doty resigned as director of the Currier in 1987. Continuing his active career in the arts, in 1989 he guest-curated three major exhibitions shown at the Currier: *By Good Hands: New Hampshire Folk Art*, organized with The University Art Galleries of the University of New Hampshire; *Varujan Boghosian: A Retrospective*, organized for the Hood Museum of Art, Dartmouth College; and a retrospective on American painter John Button.

THE NEW PAVILIONS

The most visible accomplishment of Doty's tenure was the building of the museum's new wings. The need for expansion had been determined as early as 1962, when Buckley commissioned an architect to draw up tentative plans for consideration. The hope was to build the addition in time for the museum's thirty-fifth anniversary in 1964. However, resources necessary to accomplish this dream were not yet available, and the trustees deferred the project.

By 1977, when Doty first arrived in Manchester, the Currier's burgeoning collection was facing a critical situation. The

Fig. 13 The north entrance and new pavilions of the Currier, photographed in 1989.

BILL FINNEY

museum had expanded in all directions, except physically. More space was desperately needed. In 1978 the Currier commissioned architect Michael B. Ingram to prepare a preliminary study of possible alternatives for the future growth of the museum.

The Fiftieth Anniversary Building Fund was established in 1979 to raise the money needed to build a new addition. The museum's trustees and advisory council provided leadership to the fund drive under the direction of Kimon S. Zachos, president of the board of trustees. Over three hundred volunteers worked on the campaign to raise the approximately three million dollars needed for the new construction and for the renovation of the original building. The Building Fund was supported through the generous donations of hundreds of contributors.

Two new pavilions were designed by the award-winning firm of Hardy Holzman Pfeiffer Associates of New York City, a firm well known for both its new construction projects and for renovations of historic public buildings and art museums. Hugh Hardy, the project architect, wrote:

> Because this project is an addition to a much-loved building, we believed it should represent a modulation, not a transformation, of the institution it houses. The results are a continuation of an architectural tradition, but invigorated by a contemporary sensibility.[18]

Hardy freely interpreted the vocabulary of the classical Italian design tradition, employing the Palladian arch motif as a unifying factor. The result is a pleasing symmetry, harmonious with the aesthetics of the original building.

Architect Alvin B. Corzilius was hired as the Currier's local representative on the project. The ground breaking took place on September 4, 1980. The construction, which was accomplished by Harvey Construction Company of Manchester, was completed in 1982. The Currier now had expanded gallery, storage and exhibition preparation space, and an improved auditorium. A new courtyard led to a second public entrance, designed to accommodate automobile and handicapped access.

The museum celebrated the opening of the new wings in April 1982 with the exhibition *Masterworks by Artists of New England*, which spanned three hundred years of New England history through works borrowed from public and private collections.

The pavilions increased the Currier's exhibition space by 60 percent, and allowed for the showing of large-scale works that could not be displayed properly in the original galleries. The ultraviolet-filtered sunlight from the skylights and generous windows provide balanced illumination in the two new galleries.

The final phase of the museum expansion was the renovation of the original building. This project started in 1982

BOB RAICHE

Fig. 14 Director Marilyn F. Hoffman, right, and guest curator Robert M.
Doty work with Vicki C. Wright, director of the University Art
Galleries, University of New Hampshire, Durham, on the sixti-
eth anniversary exhibition of New Hampshire folk art, 1989.

under the direction of curator Philip Zimmerman, with Corzilius and Frederick L. Matuszewski as consulting architects.
Repairs were done to the outside of the building, inside lighting
improvements made, and the wooden floors were refinished.
The galleries were repainted with new colors to complement
the special qualities of the collections. New display cases were
constructed for silver, pewter and glass.

The reinstallation of the permanent collection in new set-
tings designed by Zimmerman was completed in June 1983.
The collection could now be shown to better advantage and
many works which had been relegated to storage due to lack of
gallery space were now on view. The summer exhibition, *The*

Murray Collection of Glass: The Aesthetics of a Technological Revolution, organized by Zimmerman, was installed in the east pavilion to inaugurate the reinstallation, and an illustrated catalogue of the Murray Collection was edited by Zimmerman.

Over the years ornamental shrubbery and flowering trees were planted and replaced on the museum's grounds, developing a mature landscape which reflects the changing New England seasons. Landscape architect Leon Pearson created the landscaping for the new pavilions to provide an aesthetic continuation of the original grounds design. Pearson and his wife donated the new landscaping in memory of their daughter, Ann Carol Pearson.

In 1980, the Currier purchased a Victorian mansion located across the street from the museum to its northwest, in anticipation of the need for additional space. The house, designed in an Italian-villa style, was built around 1869 by Alpheus Gay, a building contractor and mayor of Manchester in 1875–1876. Guided by a study conducted by the Society for the Preservation of New England Antiquities, museum staff supervised repairs to the building. At present, part of the house is being used as an office and library annex for the museum. The Alpheus Gay House is listed on the National Register of Historic Places.

THE DIRECTORSHIP OF
MARILYN F. HOFFMAN
1988 - PRESENT

The Currier's present director, Marilyn Friedman Hoffman, is building upon the work of her predecessors and facing new challenges. The operating expense for the Currier's first full year, 1930, was less than $11,000. The full-time and part-time staff was comprised of the director, the museum secretary, two caretakers and miscellaneous "attendants and other labor." Hoffman's task today is to manage a museum which operates on an annual budget of over $1.3 million, with a full- and part-time staff of over 40 people.

To help meet these challenges, Hoffman selected Michael K. Komanecky as the Currier's fourth curator. Komanecky was educated at the State University of New York at Stony Brook and at Brown University. His museum experience includes seven years at the Yale University Art Gallery in New Haven, Connecticut. Komanecky edited a second edition of the *Handbook of the Collection* in 1990.

Through purchase and gift, the Currier's collections continue to grow. Recent acquisitions include a handsome painted chest made in 1729 by Robert Crosman, received as a gift from Marjorie Park Swope; *St. Martin on Horseback*, a medieval polychrome wood sculpture from Germany purchased through Friends funds and the Florence Andrews Todd fund; *Nydia, The Blind Girl of Pompeii*, a marble sculpture by Randolph Rogers, acquired through the Henry Melville Fuller fund; *Reminiscence of the Catskill Clove*, 1858, an oil painting by Asher B. Durand, given by Henry Melville Fuller; an 1871 inlaid-wood cabinet by Herter Brothers of New York City, purchased through Friends funds; and an eighteenth-century New Hampshire tall clock by Jacob Jones, purchased with funds given by many donors.

After 26 years of initiating and guiding the development of the education department, Marian D. Woodruff left the museum in 1988. Nancy B. Tieken was named the new director of education in 1989. In addition to providing explanatory labels for the works of art from the permanent collection on exhibition,[19] Tieken reinstated the Manchester fifth-grade school visit program and continues the family events, lectures, scholarly symposia, and films.

The Currier exhibition program continues to focus on the areas on which the Currier has built its reputation, and the museum continues to break new ground by presenting historical surveys, retrospectives of national interest, and juried exhibitions supporting both emerging and established artists from the region. The Currier continues to lend art works to major museums, including the Louvre in Paris, the Hermitage in Leningrad, and the Vatican Museums in Rome.

Today the Currier is organizing an exhibition of national importance, *Corot to Monet: The Rise of Landscape Painting in France: 1830–1870*. This will be the first major showing since 1962 focusing on the Barbizon school, and will provide a re-examination of these works through the eyes of a new generation of scholars. The exhibition will travel to New York and Dallas in 1991 and Atlanta in 1992. The Currier has begun the planning process for a project which will preserve its great collections for future generations: a climate-control system will be installed. Finally, the Currier is looking forward to the opening of the Isadore J. and Lucille Zimmerman House, scheduled for October 1990.

THE ISADORE J. AND LUCILLE ZIMMERMAN HOUSE

In 1950, two Manchester residents, Dr. Isadore J. Zimmerman and his wife Lucille Cummings Zimmerman, commissioned the renowned American architect Frank Lloyd Wright (1867–1959) to design a house for them. Their home in Manchester, with its Wright-designed furniture and gardens, is a classic example of Wright's Usonian style of domestic architecture. The house was completed in 1952.

Dr. Zimmerman was a physician on the staff of Manchester's Sacred Heart Hospital.[20] Mrs. Zimmerman was a nurse

LAURIER C. DURETTE

Fig. 15   The Isadore J. and Lucille Zimmerman House designed by Frank
Lloyd Wright, photographed in 1954.

who worked with her husband. They were major benefactors of
the Currier, providing financial support to the Fiftieth Anniversary Building Fund and regular purchase funds for the acquisition of modern sculpture. Mrs. Zimmerman served as a
museum volunteer and a member of the Advisory Council.

Recognizing the importance of their home as a work of
art, the Zimmermans decided it would eventually become a part
of the permanent collection of The Currier Gallery of Art. They
first discussed their ideas with the museum's trustees in the late
1950s. The dialogue continued over the next several years.
Kimon S. Zachos, who became president of the trustees in 1976,
guided the discussions for many years and became a close friend
of the Zimmermans.

The Zimmermans made provisions for the house and its

contents, including their fine collection of ceramics and sculpture, to be bequeathed to the Currier. They also provided a generous endowment toward the restoration, maintenance and operation of the house.

Dr. Zimmerman died in 1984. Mrs. Zimmerman transferred ownership of the house to the museum in 1985, retaining life tenancy. She passed away in March 1988, and the house officially entered the museum's collection in April 1988.

At present, the Isadore J. and Lucille Zimmerman House is undergoing restoration and conservation under the direction of curator Michael K. Komanecky. When opened as a house-museum for group tours, it will be the only Wright-designed structure available for public viewing in New England. The Zimmerman House is listed on the National Register of Historic Places.

PATRONAGE

The Currier's permanent collection has grown through the generosity of many private donors. From its earliest years, the Currier has had the good fortune of receiving outstanding works through gift and bequest, and many pieces have come into the collection through purchase funds given to the museum. Among the special purchase funds established have been the Norwin S. Bean fund, Rosmond deKalb fund, Alonzo Elliott fund, Mabel Putney Folsom fund, Jennie F. Fracker fund, Ralph W. Fracker fund, Friends of the Currier Gallery of Art fund, Henry Melville Fuller fund, Hassam and Speicher fund, Richard J. Healey fund, Marston Heard fund, Ruth W. Higgins Memorial fund, George A. Leighton fund, Murray Glass fund, Inez M. Olney fund, Print Endowment fund, Donn Purvis Memorial fund, H. Ellis Straw fund, Florence Andrews Todd fund, Nora Unwin fund, Vallarino Purchase fund, and Isadore J. and Lucille Zimmerman fund.

Through the excellent management of the original Currier endowment by the early trustees, the museum was able to weather the financial effects of the Great Depression and World War II without actively soliciting cash contributions. As the museum grew, the Currier endowment gradually became inadequate to handle all of the necessary expenses, and the need for additional funding sources became clear. The Friends of The Currier Gallery of Art program was established in 1958, primarily to raise money for the purchase of American art, and fundraising was done in the 1960s to support particular projects. The first major private contribution to the endowment fund came in 1965 with a bequest of $25,000 from the estate of Currier trustee, Mary C. Manning.

In 1972 the museum set out a voluntary contribution box at the museum entrance and began in many other ways to actively solicit funds. During the 1970s the Currier sought grants from government agencies and other sources, and also joined Federated Arts of Greater Manchester in 1976, as one of nine Manchester arts organizations receiving part of their funding through this umbrella organization.

The Fiftieth Anniversary Building Fund, started in 1979, became the museum's first concerted effort to raise a large sum of money, and it was an enormous success. The experience of implementing the Building Fund Drive increased awareness of the Currier's ongoing need to develop funding sources. In 1986 the museum established a full-time development office to handle all fundraising activities. The first director of development was Amanda Preston (1986–1989). She was followed in 1990 by Johanna Gurland. A development committee was established with trustee Robert P. Bass, Jr., as chairman. All the trustees, led by president Kimon S. Zachos, have worked actively to raise money for the museum.

Today, in addition to receiving income from investment

of its endowment, the Currier receives funding from government agencies; corporations and businesses; foundations and trusts; community, professional and educational organizations; bequests and estates; individuals and families; and memorial, honorary and planned gifts. In 1988 the Memorial Concert fund and the Maggie Rix Flower fund were initiated. The following year the Anna Stearns fund was received, which is used for the decorative arts. In early 1990, the Adelaide Dodge bequest was accepted. These funds and other sources are essential for the Currier to continue to operate as the major independent art museum in the state, and to continue to provide exhibitions and programming for the public.

Manchester, April 16, 1990.

AURORE DIONNE EATON *is a freelance writer from Manchester, New Hampshire. She earned a bachelor of fine arts degree from Colby-Sawyer College in New London, has studied theatre and film at Dartmouth College and drawing and photography at the Manchester Institute of Arts and Sciences, and is a former public relations coordinator for the Currier.*

1. Moody Currier, excerpt from "Tell Him I'll Wake Again," in *Early Poems*, printed for private circulation by Mirror Press, Manchester, 1880, and reprinted by John B. Clarke, Manchester, 1881.

2. *The Currier Gallery of Art - Manchester - New Hampshire*, booklet produced by Cram and Ferguson, architects, Boston, MA, printed by Thomas Todd Co., Boston, MA, 1921.

3. Douglass Shand Tucci, "First Impressions on the Rediscovery of Two New England Galleries by Ralph Adams Cram," The Currier Gallery of Art, *Bulletin*, Fall, 1979.

4. R. Clipston Sturgis, notes in The Currier Gallery of Art archives, dated December 10, 1923 and April 18, 1924.

5. "Works of Renowned Artist On Display Until Aug. 27," *The Leader*, Manchester, August 2, 1938.

6. Maud Briggs Knowlton, "Annual Report 1933."

7. Maud Briggs Knowlton, "Annual Report of the Director of The Currier Gallery of Art for 1932."

8. Maud Briggs Knowlton, "Annual Report 1933."

9. Minutes of the meeting of The Currier Gallery of Art board of trustees, April 15, 1930.

10. Maud Briggs Knowlton, "Annual Report of the Director of The Currier Gallery of Art for 1932."

11. The Currier Gallery of Art, *Bulletin*, October, 1942.

12. L. Ashton Thorp, *Manchester of Yesterday*, Granite State Press, Manchester, 1939, pages 265–266, 269.

13. Gordon M. Smith, "Little gallery on big scale," *Art News*, New York, January, 1952.

14. In 1948 Gyorgy Kepes was a professor in the School of Planning of the Massachusetts Institute of Technology. In 1951 he was professor of Visual Design for MIT. In 1967 he founded the Center for Advanced Visual Studies at MIT.

15. "Tea Opens Eakins Show at Currier Gallery of Art," *Manchester Evening Leader*, Manchester, May 22, 1947.

16. "Annual Report 1973," The Currier Gallery of Art, *Bulletin*, Number 1, 1974, Manchester, 1974.

17. The exhibition was organized by Randolph Langenbach, in conjunction with preparations for the book *Amoskeag: Life and Work in an American Factory-City*, by Langenbach and Tamara K. Hareven, Pantheon Books, New York, 1978.

18. Hugh Hardy, "The Currier Gallery of Art," *Building the New Museum*, proceedings of a symposium "Art Against the Wall" held December 5, 10, 12,

1985, Suzanne Stephens, editor. The Architectural League of New York, Princeton Architectural Press, New York, 1986, pages 40–43.

19.   For information on the permanent collection and on donors to the collection, refer to the *Handbook of the Collection*, published in 1979 and revised in 1990; the Currier *Bulletin*; the labels describing work from the permanent collection displayed in the galleries; and educational materials made available to museum visitors through the Education Department. Additional information is available through museum publications held in the Currier library.

20.   In 1974 Sacred Heart Hospital merged with Notre Dame Hospital to form the Catholic Medical Center.

PRESIDENTS
OF THE BOARD OF
TRUSTEES: Tenure

Robert J. Peaslee   (D. 1936)   1918-1936
Frank P. Carpenter   (D. 1938)   1937-1938
Frank W. Sargeant   (D. 1948)   1939-1947
Peter Woodbury   (D. 1970)   1947-1969
Raymond H. Daniels   1969-1976
Kimon S. Zachos   1976-

TRUSTEES:

Arthur M. Heard   1917-1938
Herman F. Straw   1917-1929
Charles H. Manning   1917-1919
Walter M. Parker   1917-1927
Benjamin A. Kimball   1917-1920
Cyrus H. Little   1917-1926
Frank W. Sargeant   1917-1947
Albert O. Brown   1917-1937
Frank P. Carpenter   1918-1938
Robert J. Peaslee   1918-1936
Penelope W. Snow   1925-1940
Maud Briggs Knowlton   1925-1956
Norwin S. Bean   1928-1957
H. Ellis Straw   1928-1950
Clarence O. Coburn   1937-1944
Mrs. Charles B. Manning   1937-1965
Marston Heard   1939-1978
Ruth W. Higgins   1939-1971
Peter Woodbury   1939-1970
Robert P. Booth   1945-1967
Florence C. Derr   1947-1960
Raymond H. Daniels   1947-1979
Wiliam G. Saltonstall   1951-1963
Henry Wheeler, Jr.   1958-1969
Ernest A. Sweet, Jr.   1958-1979
Mrs. Lawrence W. Shirley   1962-1984
Henry M. Fuller   1964-
Kimon S. Zachos   1967-

John H. Morison   1969-
Mrs. Warren R. Hedden III   1970-
Mrs. Norman F. Milne, Jr.   1972-
Davis P. Thurber   1973-
Mrs. Peter S. Freedman   1975-
Sylvio L. Dupuis   1975-1986
Mrs. John L. Sullivan   1980-1986
James W. Griswold   1981-
Robert P. Bass, Jr.   1983-
John F. Swope   1986-
Mrs. John A. Graf   1988-
William B. Hart, Jr.   1990-

TRUSTEES EMERITI:

Raymond H. Daniels
Mrs. Lawrence W. Shirley
Mrs. John L. Sullivan

DIRECTORS:

Maud Briggs Knowlton
                        (D. 1956)   1929-1946
Gordon Mackintosh Smith
                        (D. 1979)   1946-1955
Charles Edward Buckley   1955-1964
William Hutton   1965-1968
David Stopford Brooke   1968-1977
Robert McIntyre Doty   1977-1987
Marilyn Friedman Hoffman   1988-

CURATORS:

Melvin E. Watts   1946-1981
Philip D. Zimmerman   1981-1983
Marilyn F. Hoffman   1984-1987
Michael K. Komanecky   1988-

CURATOR EMERITUS:

Melvin E. Watts